SIMPLY MODERN CHRISTMAS

simply modern
CHRISTMAS

FRESH QUILTING PATTERNS FOR THE HOLIDAYS

Cindy Lammon

Martingale®
Create with Confidence

dedication

To my granddaughters, Elyse and Madelyn, who remind me at Christmas,
and every day, to delight in the simple things in life.

Simply Modern Christmas:
Fresh Quilting Patterns for the Holidays
© 2013 by Cindy Lammon

Martingale®
19021 120th Ave. NE, Ste. 102
Bothell, WA 98011-9511 USA
ShopMartingale.com

Printed in China
18 17 16 15 14 13   8 7 6 5 4 3 2 1

Library of Congress Cataloging-in-Publication Data
is available upon request.

ISBN: 978-1-60468-218-2

CREDITS

President and CEO: Tom Wierzbicki
Editor in Chief: Mary V. Green
Design Director: Paula Schlosser
Managing Editor: Karen Costello Soltys
Acquisitions Editor: Karen M. Burns
Technical Editor: Laurie Baker
Copy Editor: Tiffany Mottet
Production Manager: Regina Girard
Cover and Interior Designer: Adrienne Smitke
Photographer: Brent Kane
Illustrator: Christine Erikson

contents

introduction

I love the Christmas holiday season and everything about it! It's a time filled with decorating, shopping, partying, eating, and creating—all of my favorite things. I also love traditions, and the Christmas season is certainly filled with them. But what if your style isn't traditional? What if your decor is simple, modern, and bright? Is there a way to maintain the traditions of the holidays but create quilts and accessories in a modern style? I think so!

I started out as a very traditional quilter. In recent years the modern quilting movement has definitely caught my eye and my heart. I'm attracted to the clean and simple yet colorful style of modern quilting. Mix all that with some traditional designs, and I think you have the perfect recipe for some fresh and modern Christmas quilts.

As more and more designer fabric becomes readily available, combining contemporary fabric with simple traditional patterns becomes a snap. The added bonus of veering away from traditional Christmas designs is that, although these projects have a Christmassy feel, you can continue to enjoy them all year round. Most of the patterns will produce a stunning quilt made up in any fabric.

I've included some very quick and easy projects, perfect for handmade gifts. A simple table runner ("Simply Simple" on page 73) and wall hanging ("Seeing Stars" on page 25) both start with a gorgeous print. In fact, many of the projects allow a focus fabric (or two) to shine. It's a pretty simple formula: Find a great print, add some coordinates, and start some modern holiday sewing!

I hope your holiday season is simple, joyful, and filled with creative moments!

basic techniques

Knowing some basic quiltmaking methods will help everything run smoothly. The following techniques are used in many of the projects in this book. You'll also find free, downloadable information on more techniques at ShopMartingale.com/HowtoQuilt.

PRESSING

If you've been quilting for a while, you're probably used to pressing seam allowances to one side. Recently the trend has changed, and many modern quilters are pressing their seam allowances open, similar to techniques used in garment making. I've come to discover that each technique has its advantage. Pressing seam allowances to one side can really help with matching seams when piecing. Pressing the seam allowances open has the advantage of flattening out the block a bit more than side-pressed seam allowances. For these reasons, I find myself using both techniques depending on the construction of the block, and you'll find both methods used throughout this book.

FLYING GEESE

A very common shape in quilt patterns, flying-geese units can sometimes be tricky to piece accurately. Rulers and techniques for making them abound in the quilting market. I've used what I consider one of the simplest and most accurate techniques, but feel free to use whatever method you prefer. The finished size can easily be calculated by taking the size of the cut rectangle and subtracting ½" from the length and height. For example, a flying-geese unit that's made from a 2½" × 4½" rectangle will finish to 2" × 4".

You'll need one rectangle and two squares for each flying-geese unit.

1. Use your preferred marking tool to draw a line from corner to corner on the wrong side of the two squares.

2. Place one of the marked squares on one end of the rectangle, right sides together and edges even, noting the direction of the drawn line. Sew directly on the drawn line. Press the square in half along the seam line, toward the upper corner. The edges of the square should line up with the rectangle. Fold the square back and trim the seam allowances to ¼" using a ruler and rotary cutter or scissors. Press the corner triangle back into place.

3. Place the second marked square on the opposite end of the rectangle, right sides together and edges even, noting the direction of the drawn line. Repeat the sewing, pressing and trimming techniques from step 2.

TRIMMING HALF-SQUARE-TRIANGLE UNITS

A square formed by sewing two half-square triangles together along the long edges is often called a half-square-triangle unit. Cutting the triangles oversized and then trimming the resulting square to the required dimensions will result in perfectly sized half-square-triangle units.

1. Sew the triangles together along the long edges.

2. Align the 45° diagonal line of a square ruler over the seam line. Keep the marking for the finished-size unit within the lower-left corner of the unit. Trim the first two sides.

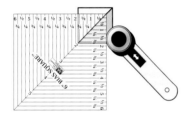

3. Rotate the unit and align the ruler markings for the finished-size unit with the trimmed edges in the lower-left corner. Trim the remaining two sides.

QUILT BACKING

One of the latest trends in modern quilting is creating quilt backings from leftover fabrics from quilt tops, with the addition of some extra yardage. In each of these patterns, I've given you yardage for making a backing from one piece of fabric. But it can often be more economical (and a great way of using excess fabric scraps) to free-form piece your fabrics together.

A simple backing pieced with excess yardage from "Coming Together" (page 75).

Calculating the fabric requirements is easy with a rough sketch. Draw a square or rectangle representing the size of the backing piece you're aiming for. Start with the largest piece of fabric you're working with and draw in where it will go, adding the dimensions to the diagram. I often purchase a piece that will fill the width or the length of the backing. Continue drawing, filling in the remaining pieces and noting the dimensions. Then be sure to add ½" to each piece for seam allowances. It's also fun to add an extra block or two to your backing.

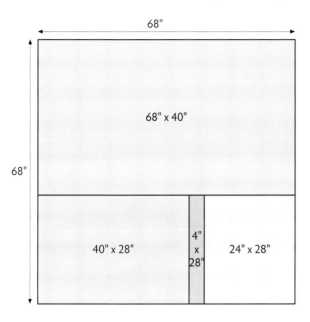

68"

68"

68" x 40"

40" x 28"

4"
x
28"

24" x 28"

peppermint float

Pieced and machine quilted by Cindy Lammon

Finished quilt: 53" x 53" ∗ **Finished block: 12" x 12"**

I love how these holiday stars appear to be floating on the frames. All it takes is some simple piecing to create an interesting illusion.

MATERIALS

Yardage is based on 42"-wide fabric. Fat quarters measure 18" x 21". Fat eighths measure 9" x 21".

4 fat quarters of assorted red prints for blocks

4 fat quarters of assorted green prints for blocks

⅞ yard of white-and-black floral for sashing

¾ yard of black-and-red floral for outer border

⅔ yard of black-and-white polka-dot fabric for block frames

⅝ yard of white solid for block backgrounds

⅝ yard of red-and-white diagonal-striped fabric for center block and binding

⅜ yard of white-and-black polka-dot fabric for blocks

⅓ yard of green tone-on-tone fabric for inner border

⅛ yard of black-and-white houndstooth fabric for cornerstones

1 fat eighth of black print for block

3⅝ yards of fabric for backing

59" x 59" piece of batting

13

CUTTING

From the white-and-black polka-dot fabric, cut:

2 strips, 3½" × 42"; crosscut into 36 rectangles, 2" × 3½"

2 strips, 2" × 42"; crosscut into 36 squares, 2" × 2"

From *each* of the 4 green and 4 red fat quarters, cut:

8 squares, 2" × 2" (32 green and 32 red *total*)

1 square, 3½" × 3½" (4 green and 4 red *total*)

4 squares, 3⅞" × 3⅞"; cut each square in half diagonally to yield 8 triangles (32 green and 32 red *total*)

From the black-print fat eighth, cut:

8 squares, 2" × 2"

1 square, 3½" × 3½"

From the red-and-white diagonal-striped fabric, cut:

4 squares, 3⅞" × 3⅞"; cut *each* square in half diagonally to yield 8 triangles

6 binding strips, 2½" × 42"

From the white solid, cut:

3 strips, 2½" × 42"; crosscut into 36 squares, 2½" × 2½"

2 strips, 5¼" × 42"; crosscut into 9 squares, 5¼" × 5¼". Cut *each* square into quarters diagonally to yield 36 triangles.

From the black-and-white polka-dot fabric, cut:

13 strips, 1½" × 42"; crosscut into:
    36 rectangles, 1½" × 7¼"
    36 rectangles, 1½" × 3½"
    36 rectangles, 1½" × 2½"

From the white-and-black floral, cut:

2 strips, 12½" × 42"; crosscut into 24 rectangles, 2½" × 12½"

From the black-and-white houndstooth fabric, cut:

1 strip, 2½" × 42"; crosscut into 16 squares, 2½" × 2½"

From the green tone-on-tone fabric, cut:

5 strips, 1½" × 42"

From the black-and-red floral, cut:

6 strips, 3¾" × 42"

MAKING THE BLOCKS

After sewing each seam, press the seam allowances in the direction indicated by the arrows.

1. Refer to "Flying Geese" on page 9 to make four flying-geese units using the white-and-black polka-dot 2" × 3½" rectangles and pairs of matching green 2" squares.

Make 4.

2. Arrange the flying-geese units from step 1, a matching green 3½" square, and four white-and-black polka-dot 2" squares into three horizontal rows as shown. Sew the pieces in each row together; press. Join the rows to complete the block center; press.

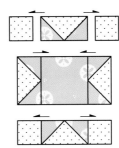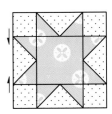

3. Trim both ends of each black-and-white polka-dot 1½" × 7¼" rectangle, aligning the 45° line on the ruler with the rectangle long edge as shown, to create trapezoids.

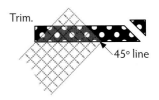

Trim.

45° line

4. Sew a trapezoid from step 3 to a white triangle; press. Make four.

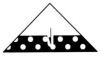

Make 4.

Sewing a Trapezoid to a Triangle

Find the center of both the triangle and the trapezoid by folding them in half and finger creasing the fold. Line up the pieces as shown, matching the centers. You'll notice that the points of the triangle, also known as "dog-ears," show on each side.

Center

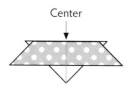

5. Choose eight matching red triangles. Sew one to the side of each triangle unit from step 4; press. Sew another red triangle to the opposite side and press. Make four outer star-point units.

Make 4.

6. Sew a black-and-white polka-dot 1½" × 2½" rectangle to a white 2½" square; press. Sew a black-and-white polka-dot 1½" × 3½" rectangle to the adjacent side of the square; press. Make four corner units.

Make 4.

7. Arrange the block center unit from step 2, the four outer star-point units from step 5, and the four corner units from step 6 in three horizontal rows as shown. Sew the units in each row together; press. Join the rows; press.

8. Repeat steps 1–7 to make a total of four blocks with green center stars and red outer stars, using the red-and-white striped triangles for one block. In the same manner, make four blocks with red center stars and green outer stars, and one block with a black center star and a red outer star.

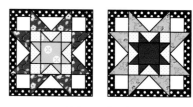

Make 4 of each.

Make 1.

ASSEMBLING THE QUILT TOP

1. Refer to the quilt assembly diagram below to arrange the blocks, the white-and-black floral 2½" × 12½" sashing strips, and the black-and-white houndstooth 2½" cornerstones as shown. Sew the sashing strips and cornerstones in each sashing row together. Press the seam allowances toward the sashing strips. Sew the blocks and sashing strips in each block row together. Press the seam allowances toward the sashing strips. Alternately join the sashing rows and block rows. Press the seam allowances in one direction.

2. Sew the five green tone-on-tone 1½"-wide strips together end to end to make one long strip. From the pieced strip, cut two strips the length of the quilt top. Sew the strips to the sides of the quilt top. Press the seam allowances toward the border. From the remainder of the pieced strip, cut two strips the width of the quilt top. Sew these strips to the top and bottom of the quilt top. Press the seam allowances toward the border.

3. Repeat step 2 with the black-and-red floral 3¾"-wide strips for the outer border.

FINISHING THE QUILT

Layer and baste the top, batting, and backing together. Quilt as desired. Bind the quilt using the red-and-white striped 2½"-wide strips.

Quilt assembly

Peppermint Float

joy

Pieced by Cindy Lammon; machine quilted by Candy Grisham

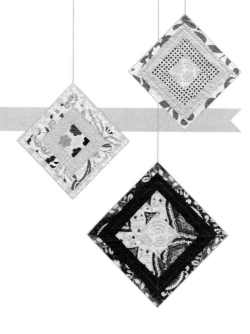

Finished quilt: 68" x 82¼" ∗ **Finished block: 10" x 10"**

Joy is defined as a feeling of great pleasure and happiness—certainly a feeling we long for during the holidays and all year long. For some reason, piecing together a pile of colorful strips and scraps brings me a bit of joy. I hope it does the same for you!

MATERIALS

Yardage is based on 42"-wide fabric. Fat quarters measure 18" x 21".

20 fat quarters of assorted red, green, and aqua prints for blocks

2⅛ yards of white solid for blocks and setting triangles

1⅝ yards of large-scale floral for blocks and outer border

⅜ yard of aqua tone-on-tone fabric for inner border

⅔ yard of multicolor-striped fabric for binding

5½ yards of fabric for backing

74" × 88" piece of batting

17

CUTTING

From *each* of the 20 assorted-print fat quarters, cut:

1 strip, 2" × 21" (20 total); crosscut into:
    2 rectangles, 2" × 3½" (40 total)
    2 rectangles, 2" × 6½" (40 total)
2 strips, 1¾" × 21" (40 total); crosscut *each* strip into:
    1 rectangle, 1¾" × 6½" (40 total)
    1 rectangle, 1¾" × 9" (40 total)
2 strips, 1¼" × 21" (40 total); crosscut *each* strip into:
    1 rectangle, 1¼" × 9" (40 total)
    1 rectangle, 1¼" × 10½" (40 total)
1 square, 3½" × 3½" (20 total)

From the large-scale floral, cut:

2 strips, 5½" × 42"; crosscut into 12 squares,
    5½" × 5½"
8 strips, 5" × 42"

From the white solid, cut:

12 strips, 3" × 42"; crosscut *each* strip into:
    2 rectangles, 3" × 5½" (24 total)
    2 rectangles, 3" × 10½" (24 total)
2 strips, 15⅜" × 42"; crosscut *each* strip into 2
    squares, 15⅜" × 15⅜". Cut *each* square into
    quarters diagonally to yield 16 side setting
    triangles (you'll have 2 left over).
2 squares, 8" × 8"; cut *each* square in half diagonally
    to yield 4 corner setting triangles

From the aqua tone-on-tone fabric, cut:

7 strips, 1½" × 42"

From the multicolor-striped fabric, cut:

8 binding strips, 2½" × 42"

MAKING THE SQUARE-IN-A-SQUARE BLOCKS

After sewing each seam, press the seam allowances in the direction indicated by the arrows, or press the seam allowances open.

1. Sort the pieces cut from the fat quarters into 20 piles, one for each block. Each pile should include the following:

Center: 1 square, 3½" × 3½"
First round: 1 matching set of 2 rectangles,
    2" × 3½", and 2 rectangles, 2" × 6½"
Second round: 1 matching set of 2 rectangles,
    1¾" × 6½", and 2 rectangles, 1¾" × 9"
Third round: 1 matching set of 2 rectangles,
    1¼" × 9", and 2 rectangles, 1¼" × 10½"

2. Select one set of pieces. Sew the 2" × 3½" rectangles to opposite sides of the center square; press. Sew the matching 2" × 6½" rectangles to the top and bottom of the square; press.

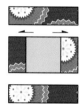

3. Refer to step 2 to sew the 1¾" × 6½" rectangles and the matching 1¾" × 9" rectangles to the unit from step 2.

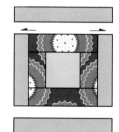 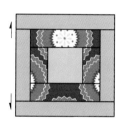

4. Refer to step 2 to sew the 1¼" × 9" rectangles and the matching 1¼" × 10½" rectangles to the unit from step 3.

5. Repeat steps 2–4 to make a total of 20 blocks.

MAKING THE ALTERNATE BLOCKS

Sew white 3" × 5½" rectangles to opposite sides of a floral 5½" square; press. Sew white 3" × 10½" rectangles to the top and bottom of the square; press. Repeat to make a total of 12 blocks.

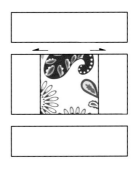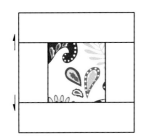

Make 12.

ASSEMBLING THE QUILT TOP

1. Refer to the quilt assembly diagram below to arrange the blocks in diagonal rows as shown. Add the white side setting triangles along the sides and the white corner setting triangles to the corners. Sew the blocks and side setting triangles in each row together. Press the seam allowances toward the Square-in-a-Square blocks. Join the rows. Press the seam allowances away from the center row. Add the corner triangles last. Press the seam allowances toward the triangles.

2. Sew the seven aqua tone-on-tone 1½"-wide strips together end to end to make one long strip. From the pieced strip, cut two strips the length of the quilt top. Sew the strips to the sides of the quilt top. Press the seam allowances toward the border. From the remainder of the pieced strip, cut two strips the width of the quilt top. Sew these strips to the top and bottom of the quilt top. Press the seam allowances toward the border.

3. Repeat step 2 with the floral 5"-wide strips for the outer border.

FINISHING THE QUILT

Layer and baste the top, batting, and backing together. Quilt as desired. Bind the quilt using the multicolor-striped 2½"-wide strips.

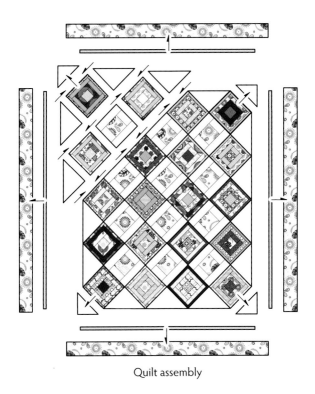

Quilt assembly

argyle

Pieced and machine quilted by Cindy Lammon

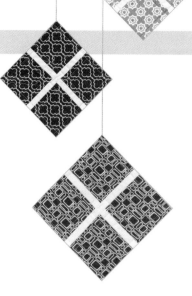

Finished quilt: 60½" x 80½" ∗ Finished block: 7" x 7"

I've never seen an Argyle pattern that I didn't love. Argyle sweaters just evoke a warm, cozy feeling— sitting by the fireplace, reading a book, and playing a game with friends and family are the perfect activities when wearing one. How about an Argyle quilt to add to the coziness? It would be a great gift for that man, big or little, in your life.

MATERIALS

Yardage is based on 42"-wide fabric. Fat quarters measure 18" x 21".

1⅓ yards of black-and-white houndstooth fabric for setting triangles and binding

1⅓ yards of green tone-on-tone fabric for outer border

5 fat quarters of assorted red prints for blocks

5 fat quarters of assorted green prints for blocks

1¼ yards of gray print for alternate blocks

⅞ yard of white solid for blocks

¼ yard of red solid for inner border

5½ yards of fabric for backing

67" x 87" piece of batting

CUTTING

From the white solid, cut:

3 strips, 3¾" × 42"; crosscut into 118 rectangles, 1" × 3¾"

2 strips, 7½" × 42"; crosscut into 59 rectangles, 1" × 7½"

From *each of 3* of the assorted red fat quarters, cut:

4 strips, 3¾" × 21" (12 total); crosscut *each* strip into 4 squares, 3¾" × 3¾" (48 total)

From *each of the remaining* 2 assorted red fat quarters, cut:

3 strips, 3¾" × 21" (6 total); crosscut *each* strip into 4 squares, 3¾" × 3¾" (24 total)

From *each of 2* of the assorted green fat quarters, cut:

4 strips, 3¾" × 21" (8 total); crosscut *each* strip into 4 squares, 3¾" × 3¾" (32 total)

From *each of the remaining 3* assorted green fat quarters, cut:

3 strips, 3¾" × 21" (9 total); crosscut *each* strip into 4 squares, 3¾" × 3¾" (36 total)

From the gray print, cut:

10 strips, 3¾" × 42"; crosscut into 96 squares, 3¾" × 3¾"

From the black-and-white houndstooth fabric, cut:

5 squares, 11⅛" × 11⅛"; cut into quarters diagonally to yield 20 side setting triangles

2 squares, 5⅞" × 5⅞"; cut in half diagonally to yield 4 corner setting triangles

8 binding strips, 2½" × 42"

From the red solid, cut:

7 strips, 1" × 42"

From the green tone-on-tone fabric, cut:

8 strips, 5" × 42"

MAKING THE BLOCKS

After sewing each seam, press the seam allowances in the direction indicated by the arrows.

1. Select four matching red 3¾" squares. Sew a white 1" × 3¾" rectangle between two squares; press. Make two.

Make 2.

2. Sew a white 1" × 7½" rectangle between the two units from step 1; press.

3. Repeat steps 1 and 2 with the remaining red and green 3¾" squares to make a total of 18 red blocks and 17 green blocks.

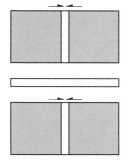

Make 18.   Make 17.

4. Repeat steps 1 and 2 with the gray 3¾" squares to make 24 gray blocks, pressing the seam allowances toward the white rectangles.

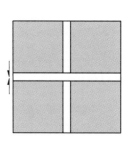

Make 24.

ASSEMBLING THE QUILT TOP

1. Refer to the quilt assembly diagram below to arrange the blocks in diagonal rows as shown. Add the houndstooth side setting triangles along the sides and the houndstooth corner triangles to the corners. Sew the blocks and side setting triangles in each row together. Press the seam allowances toward the gray blocks and setting triangles. Join the rows; press the seam allowances away from the center row. Add the corner triangles last. Press the seam allowances toward the triangles.

2. Sew the seven red-solid 1"-wide strips together end to end to make one long strip. From the pieced strip, cut two strips the length of the quilt top. Sew the strips to the sides of the quilt top. Press the seam allowances toward the border. From the remainder of the pieced strip, cut two strips the width of the quilt top. Sew these strips to the top and bottom of the quilt top. Press the seam allowances toward the border.

3. Repeat step 2 with the green tone-on-tone 5"-wide strips for the outer border.

FINISHING THE QUILT

Layer and baste the top, batting, and backing together. Quilt as desired. Bind the quilt using the black-and-white houndstooth 2½"-wide strips.

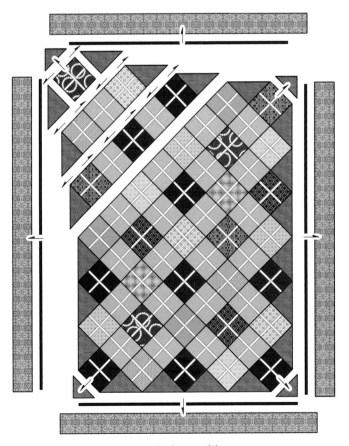

Quilt assembly

Argyle

seeing stars

Pieced and machine quilted by Cindy Lammon

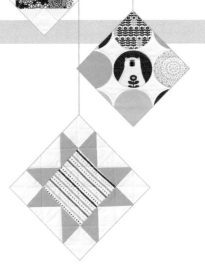

Finished quilt: 40½" x 40½" * Finished block: 8" x 8"

When you find a beautiful, large-scale print or novelty print, don't you just want to show it off? Here's the perfect little project for that! Make your focus fabric the star by placing it right in the center of this wall hanging or table topper.

MATERIALS

Yardage is based on 42"-wide fabric. Fat quarters measure 18" x 21".

⅝ yard of white solid for background

⅝ yard of large-scale print for center square

⅝ yard of teal-and-red print for border*

½ yard of teal tone-on-tone fabric for star points

¼ yard of teal-and-red striped fabric for star centers

¼ yard of red print for alternate block centers

½ yard of red solid for binding

2 yards of fabric for pieced backing

46" x 46" piece of batting

Be sure your fabric is at least 41"-wide after washing. If not, purchase ¾ yard.

CUTTING

From the white solid, cut:

3 strips, 4½" × 42"; crosscut into 48 rectangles, 2½" × 4½"

2 strips, 2½" × 42"; crosscut into 32 squares, 2½" × 2½"

From the teal tone-on-tone fabric, cut:

6 strips, 2½" × 42"; crosscut into 96 squares, 2½" × 2½"

From the teal-and-red striped fabric, cut:

1 strip, 4½" × 42"; crosscut into 8 squares, 4½" × 4½"

From the red print, cut:

1 strip, 4½" × 42"; crosscut into 8 squares, 4½" × 4½"

From the large-scale print, cut:

1 square, 16½" × 16½"

From the teal-and-red print, cut:

4 strips, 4½" × 42"

From the backing fabric, cut:

1 rectangle, 40½" × 48½"

2 rectangles, 8½" × 24½"

From the red solid, cut:

5 binding strips, 2½" × 42"

MAKING THE STAR BLOCKS

After sewing each seam, press the seam allowances in the direction indicated by the arrows.

1. Refer to "Flying Geese" on page 9 to make 48 flying-geese units using the white 2½" × 4½" rectangles and teal tone-on-tone 2½" squares.

Make 48.

2. Arrange four flying-geese units from step 1, one teal-and-red striped 4½" square, and four white 2½" squares into three horizontal rows as shown. Sew the pieces in each row together; press. Join the rows to complete the

block; press. Repeat to make a total of eight Star blocks. Set the remaining flying-geese units aside for the alternate blocks.

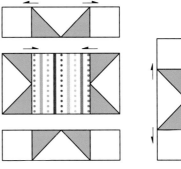
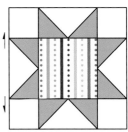

Make 8.

MAKING THE ALTERNATE BLOCKS

Sew two of the remaining flying-geese units to opposite sides of a red 4½" square; press. Repeat to make a total of eight alternate blocks.

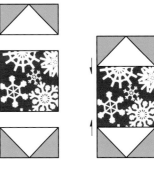

Make 8.

ASSEMBLING THE QUILT TOP

1. Sew two alternate blocks and one Star block together as shown; press. Repeat to make a total of two rows.

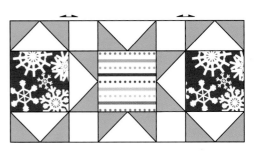

Make 2.

2. Sew three Star blocks and two alternate blocks together as shown; press. Repeat to make a total of two rows.

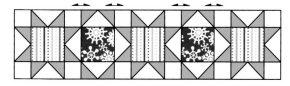

Make 2.

3. Refer to the quilt assembly diagram below to sew the rows from step 1 to opposite sides of the large-scale print 16½" square; press. Sew the rows from step 2 to the top and bottom of the square; press.

4. Trim two teal-and-red print 4½"-wide strips to the length of the quilt top and sew them to the sides of the quilt top; press the seam allowances toward the border strips. Trim the remaining two teal-and-red print strips to the width of the quilt top and sew them to the top and bottom of the quilt top; press.

FINISHING THE QUILT

1. Sew the backing pieces together as shown.

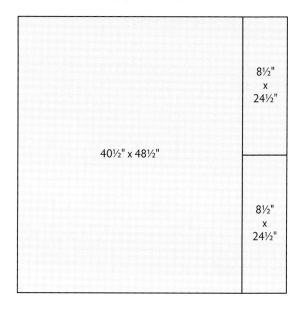

2. Layer and baste the top, batting, and backing together. Quilt as desired. Bind the quilt using the red-solid 2½"-wide strips.

Quilt assembly

funky christmas

Pieced and quilted by Cindy Lammon

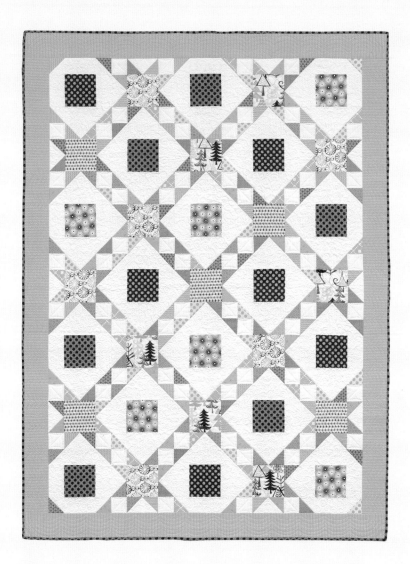

Finished quilt: 58½" x 78½" * **Finished block: 10" x 10"**

Funky—modern and stylish in an unconventional way. I think it's the perfect description for this traditional quilt block, made fun and funky by the use of nontraditional color choices.

MATERIALS

Yardage is based on 42"-wide fabric. Fat quarters measure 18" x 21".

2⅞ yards of white solid for background

1 yard of aqua-and-white striped fabric for borders

7 fat quarters of assorted aqua prints for blocks

3 fat quarters of assorted red-and-pink prints for blocks

3 fat quarters of assorted Christmas prints for blocks

⅔ yard of red-and-pink polka-dot fabric for binding

5¼ yards of fabric for backing

65" × 85" piece of batting

CUTTING

From the white solid, cut:

8 strips, 5½" × 42"; crosscut into 104 rectangles,
   3" × 5½"

6 strips, 3" × 42"; crosscut into 68 squares, 3" × 3"

3 strips, 10½" × 42"; crosscut into 36 rectangles,
   3" × 10½"

From *each* of the 7 aqua print fat quarters, cut:

5 strips, 3" × 21" (35 total); crosscut into 30 squares,
   3" × 3" (210 total; you'll have 2 left over)

From *each* of the 3 Christmas print fat quarters, cut:

2 strips, 5½" × 21" (6 total); crosscut into 6 squares,
   5½" × 5½" (18 total; you'll have 1 left over)

From *each* of the 3 red-and-pink fat quarters, cut:

2 strips, 5½" × 21" (6 total); crosscut into 6 squares,
   5½" × 5½" (18 total)

From the aqua-and-white striped fabric, cut:

7 strips, 4½" × 42"

From the red-and-pink polka-dot fabric, cut:

8 binding strips, 2½" × 42"

MAKING THE STAR BLOCKS

After sewing each seam, press the seam allowances
in the direction indicated by the arrows.

1. Refer to "Flying Geese" on page 9 to make
    a flying-geese unit using one white 3" × 5½"
    rectangle and two aqua 3" squares. Repeat to
    make a total of 68 flying-geese units.

Make 68.

2. Arrange four flying-geese units from step 1, a
    Christmas print 5½" square, and four white 3"
    squares into three horizontal rows as shown.

Sew the pieces in each row together; press.
Join the rows to complete the block; press.
Repeat to make a total of 17 Star blocks.

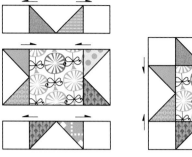
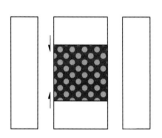
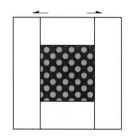

Make 17.

MAKING THE ALTERNATE BLOCKS

1. Sew white 3" × 5½" rectangles to the top and
    bottom of a red-and-pink 5½" square; press.
    Sew white 3" × 10½" rectangles to the sides
    of the unit. Repeat to make a total of 18 units.

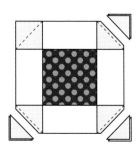

Make 18.

2. Use your preferred marker to draw a diago-
    nal line from corner to corner on the wrong
    side of each of the remaining aqua 3" squares.
    Place a marked square on each corner of a
    unit from step 1, noting the direction of the
    marked line. Sew on the marked line. Trim ¼"
    from the stitching line; press. Repeat to make
    a total of 18 alternate blocks.

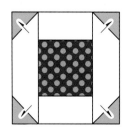

Make 18.

ASSEMBLING THE QUILT TOP

1. Refer to the quilt assembly diagram below to arrange the blocks in seven rows of five blocks each, alternating the two blocks in each row and from row to row. Sew the blocks in each row together. Press the seam allowances toward the alternate blocks. Join the rows. Press the seam allowances in one direction.

2. Join two aqua-and-white striped 4½"-wide strips together end to end to make one long strip. Repeat to make a total of two pieced strips. Trim both pieced strips to the length of the quilt top. Sew the strips to the sides of the quilt top. Press the seam allowances toward the border.

3. Sew the remaining three aqua-and-white strips together end to end to make one long strip. From the pieced strip, cut two strips to the width of the quilt top and sew them to the top and bottom of the quilt top. Press the seam allowances toward the border.

FINISHING THE QUILT

Layer and baste the top, batting, and backing together. Quilt as desired. Bind the quilt using the red-and-pink polka-dot 2½"-wide strips.

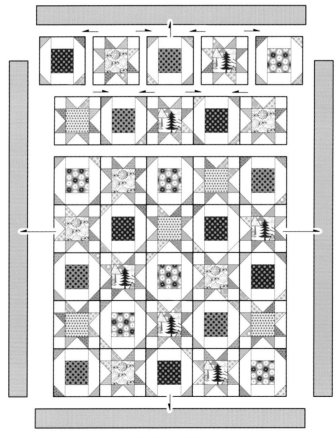

Quilt assembly

spruced up

Pieced and quilted by Cindy Lammon

Finished quilt: 55½" x 68½"

A few years ago, we replaced our Christmas tree with a tall, skinny one, hoping to save space in a smaller house. I was so happy with the look of it—more modern and sculptural. Suddenly the idea popped into my head to add a tall, skinny tree to a quilt. And this is the result! I think it's fun and whimsical. Pay close attention to the order in which the rows are pieced together, as it may be a bit different than you're used to.

MATERIALS

Yardage is based on 42"-wide fabric.

1½ yards of white-and-blue print for outer border

⅞ yard of green tone-on-tone fabric for tree appliqué

⅝ yard of red solid for inner border

½ yard of red-green-and-blue print for horizontal strip

⅜ yard of white-with-red polka dot for block and horizontal strip

⅓ yard of blue-striped fabric for block and horizontal strip

⅓ yard of red-and-green print for horizontal strip

⅓ yard of red diamond print for block and horizontal strip

¼ yard *each* of red-with-white polka dot, green-checked fabric, white print, and white-and-red print for horizontal strips

¼ yard yellow solid for block and border star

¼ yard of red tone-on-tone fabric for blocks

⅛ yard *each* of white solid and green solid for blocks

4" x 9" rectangle of brown print for tree trunk appliqué

⅝ yard of green print for binding

3⅞ yards of fabric for backing

62" x 75" piece of batting

1⅝ yards of 12"-wide paper-backed fusible web

CUTTING

From the white solid, cut:
4 rectangles, 2½" × 4½"
4 squares, 2½" × 2½"

From the red diamond print, cut:
1 strip, 4½" × 39½"
1 square, 4½" × 4½"
8 squares, 2½" × 2½"

From the red-and-green print, cut:
1 strip, 8½" × 42"; crosscut into:
    1 rectangle, 8½" × 15½"
    1 rectangle, 8½" × 16½"

From the red tone-on-tone fabric, cut:
1 square, 4½" × 4½"
4 rectangles, 2" × 3½"
8 squares, 2½" × 2½"
4 squares, 2" × 2"

From the yellow solid, cut:
1 square, 4½" × 4½"
1 square, 3½" × 3½"
2 squares, 3" × 3"; cut in half diagonally
    to yield 4 triangles
4 squares, 2½" × 2½"
8 squares, 2" × 2"

From the white-with-red polka-dot fabric, cut:
1 strip, 4½" × 35½"
4 rectangles, 3½" × 6½"
4 squares, 3½" × 3½"
1 square, 3" × 3"; cut in half diagonally to yield
    2 triangles (you'll have 1 left over)
1 rectangle, 2½" × 4½"
1 square, 2½" × 2½"

From the blue-striped fabric, cut:
1 strip, 4½" × 39½"
8 squares, 3½" × 3½"

From the red-green-and-blue print, cut:
1 strip, 6½" × 42"; crosscut into:
    1 strip, 6½" × 23½"
    1 rectangle, 4½" × 6½"
1 strip, 8½" × 42"; crosscut into:
    1 square, 8½" × 8½"
    1 strip, 8½" × 23½"

From the green-checked fabric, cut:
1 strip, 6½" × 42"; crosscut into:
    1 strip, 6½" × 23½"
    1 rectangle, 4½" × 6½"

From the green solid, cut:
4 rectangles, 2½" × 4½"
4 squares, 2½" × 2½"

From the white-and-blue print, cut:
5 strips, 6½" × 42"
1 strip, 6½" × 37½"
1 rectangle, 4½" × 12½"
1 rectangle, 2½" × 8½"
3 rectangles, 2½" × 4½"
2 squares, 2½" × 2½"
1 square, 3" × 3"; cut in half diagonally to yield
    2 triangles (you'll have 1 left over)

From the red solid, cut:
3 strips, 2½" × 42"
1 strip, 2½" × 39½"
1 strip, 2½" × 37½"
1 square, 3" × 3"; cut in half diagonally to
    yield 2 triangles
1 rectangle, 2½" × 4½"
1 square, 2½" × 2½"

From the red-with-white polka-dot fabric, cut:
1 strip, 4½" × 39½"

From the white print, cut:
1 strip, 4½" × 39½"

From the white-and-red print, cut:
1 strip, 4½" × 39½"

From the green print, cut:
7 binding strips, 2½" × 42"

ASSEMBLING THE PIECED ROWS

After sewing each seam, press the seam allowances in the direction indicated by the arrows.

Row 3

1. Refer to "Flying Geese" on page 9 to make four flying-geese units using four white 2½" × 4½" rectangles and eight red diamond-print 2½" squares.

2. Arrange the flying-geese units from step 1, a matching red diamond-print 4½" square, and four white 2½" squares into three horizontal rows as shown. Sew the pieces in each row together; press. Join the rows to complete the block.

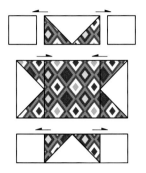 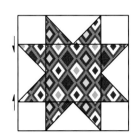

3. Refer to the quilt assembly diagram on page 39 to sew a red-and-green print 8½" × 15½" rectangle to the left side of the block. Sew a red-and-green print 8½" × 16½" rectangle to the right side of the block.

Rows 5 and 6

1. Refer to "Flying Geese" to make four flying-geese units using four red tone-on-tone 2" × 3½" rectangles and eight yellow 2" squares.

2. Arrange the flying-geese units from step 1, a yellow 3½" square, and four red tone-on-tone 2" squares into three horizontal rows as shown. Sew the pieces in each row together; press. Join the rows; press.

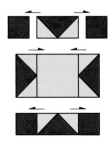 

3. Make four flying-geese units using four white-with-red polka-dot 3½" × 6½" rectangles and eight blue-striped 3½" squares.

4. Arrange the flying-geese units from step 3, the star unit from step 2, and four white-with-red polka-dot 3½" squares into three horizontal rows as shown. Sew the pieces in each row together; press. Join the rows to complete the block; press.

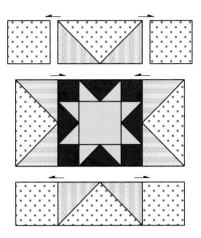

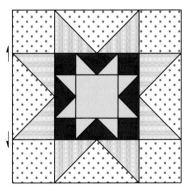

5. Sew the red-green-and-blue print and the green-checked 6½" × 23½" strips along the long edges; press the seam allowances in one direction. Refer to the quilt assembly diagram on page 39 to sew this unit to the left side of the Star block from step 4. Sew the red-green-and-blue print and the green-checked 4½" × 6½" rectangles along the short edges. Sew this unit to the right side of the Star block.

Row 9

1. Refer to "Flying Geese" to make four flying-geese units using four green-solid 2½" × 4½" rectangles and eight red tone-on-tone 2½" squares.

2. Arrange the flying-geese units from step 1, a matching red tone-on-tone 4½" square, and four green-solid 2½" squares into three horizontal rows as shown. Sew the pieces in each row together; press. Join the rows to complete the block.

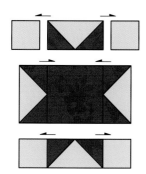

3. Sew a red-green-and-blue print 8½" square to the left side of the block. Sew a red-green-and-blue print 8½" × 23½" rectangle to the right side of the block.

Top Border and Row 1

1. Refer to "Flying Geese" to make two flying-geese units using two white-and-blue print 2½" × 4½" rectangles and four yellow 2½" squares.

Make 2.

2. Sew yellow triangles to one white-and-blue print triangle, one white-with-red polka-dot triangle, and two red-solid triangles to make

half-square-triangle units; press. Refer to "Trimming Half-Square-Triangle Units" on page 10 to trim each unit to 2½" × 2½".

Make 1.   Make 1.   Make 2.

3. Arrange the flying-geese units from step 1, the half-square-triangle units from step 2, one white-and-blue print 2½" × 8½" rectangle, two white-and-blue print 2½" squares, one yellow 4½" square, one white-with-red polka-dot 2½" square, one white-with-red polka-dot 2½" × 4½" rectangle, one red-solid 2½"square, and a white-and-blue print 2½" × 4½" rectangle into four horizontal rows as shown. Sew the pieces in each row together; press. Join the rows; press. Add the white-and-blue print 4½" × 12½" rectangle to the left side of the unit; press.

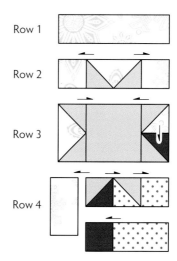

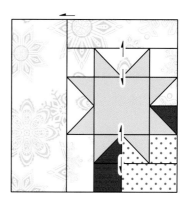

4. Sew the red-solid 2½" × 4½" rectangle to the end of the white-with-red polka-dot 4½" × 35½" strip; press. Sew the white-and-blue print 6½" × 37½" strip to the red-solid 2½" × 37½" strip; press. Sew these two strips together, keeping the red rectangle on the right side; press. Add the unit from step 3 to the left side of the pieced strip; press.

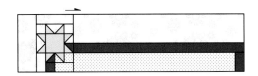

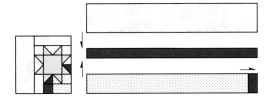

ASSEMBLING THE QUILT TOP

1. Sew rows 2–10 together as shown. Add the red-solid 2½" × 39½" inner border strip to the bottom of the pieced rows; press. Sew the three red-solid 2½" × 42" strips together end to end to make one long strip. From the pieced strip, cut two strips, 2½" × 50½". Sew these strips to the sides of the quilt center; press. Sew two white-and-blue print 6½" × 42" strips together end to end. Trim the strip to 50½" and sew it to the left side of the quilt top; press.

2. Sew the pieced top border/row 1 to the top of the quilt top; press. Sew the remaining three white-and-blue print 6½" × 42" strips together end to end. From the pieced strip, cut one strip, 6½" × 62½". Sew this to the right side of

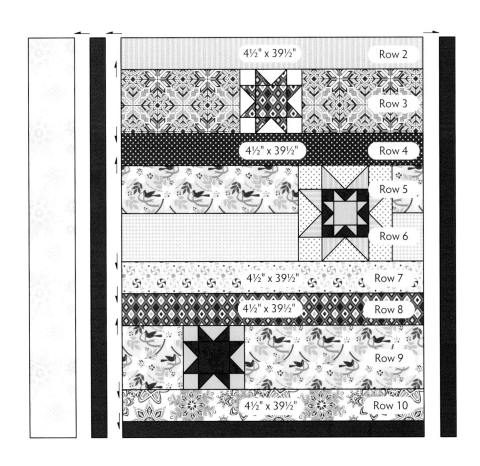

Spruced Up

the quilt top; press. Trim the remainder of the pieced strip to 6½" × 55½". Sew this strip to the bottom of the quilt top; press.

ADDING THE APPLIQUÉ

1. Using the patterns on page 41, trace one A, four B, and one C pattern onto the paper side of the fusible web. Roughly cut out each shape. Follow the manufacturer's instructions to fuse the A shape to the wrong side of

the brown print rectangle and the B and C shapes to the wrong side of the green tone-on-tone fabric. Cut out the appliqué pieces on the drawn lines.

2. Position the A piece even with the bottom red inner border, centering it on the seam line between the red inner border and the quilt center. Position the B pieces as shown, centering them on the inner red border seam line and overlapping the bottom B piece with the

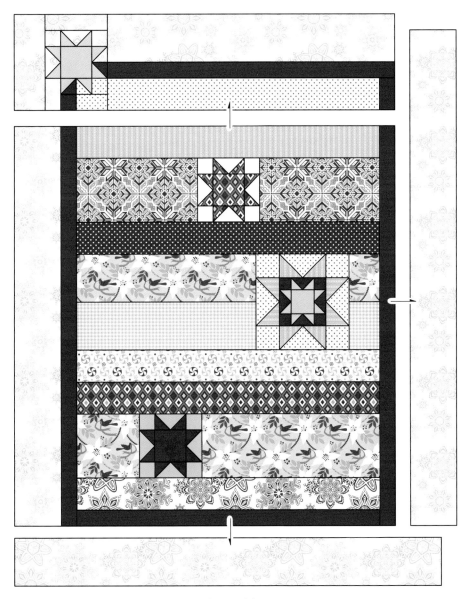

Quilt assembly

A piece as indicated by the dashed line on the pattern. Position the C piece at the top. Adjust as necessary and fuse, following the manufacturer's instructions.

3. Use your favorite machine appliqué stitch to sew the pieces in place.

FINISHING THE QUILT

Layer and baste the top, batting, and backing together. Quilt as desired. Bind the quilt using the green-print 2½"-wide strips.

Appliqué placement diagram

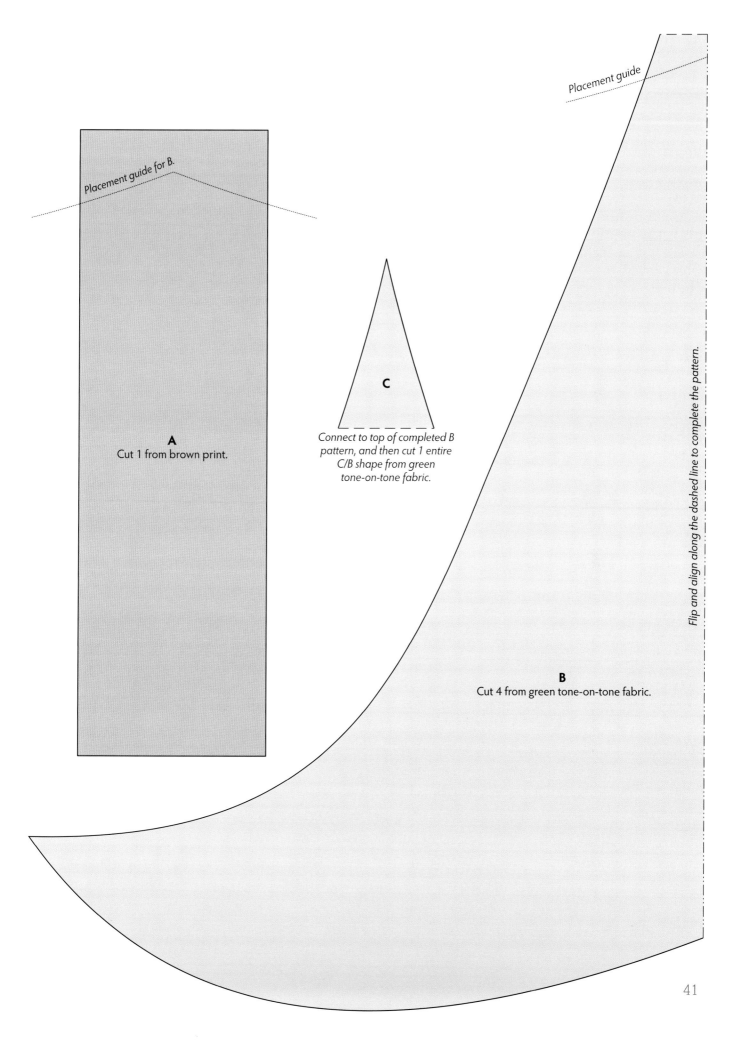

Placement guide for B.

A
Cut 1 from brown print.

C
Connect to top of completed B pattern, and then cut 1 entire C/B shape from green tone-on-tone fabric.

Placement guide

Flip and align along the dashed line to complete the pattern.

B
Cut 4 from green tone-on-tone fabric.

garden lattice

Pieced and quilted by Cindy Lammon

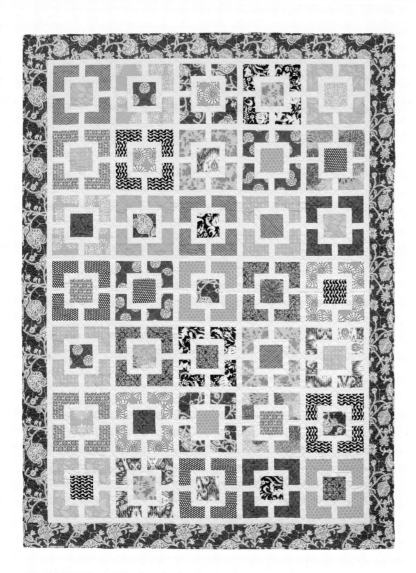

Finished quilt: 64½" x 86½" * Finished block: 10" x 10"

In my opinion, combine any shade of red with any shade of green and you have a holiday quilt. This combination of persimmon red and jade green may not scream Christmas, but it could be the perfect addition to your holiday decor. Of course, this quilt is lovely in any color combination!

MATERIALS

Yardage is based on 42"-wide fabric. Fat quarters measure 18" x 21".

17 fat quarters of assorted red, green, and black prints for blocks

2⅝ yards of cream solid for blocks, sashing, and inner border

1⅞ yards of red print for one block, outer border, and binding

5⅞ yards of fabric for backing

70" x 92" piece of batting

CUTTING

From the cream solid, cut:

3 strips, 4½" × 42"; crosscut into 70 rectangles, 1½" × 4½"

3 strips, 6½" × 42"; crosscut into 70 rectangles, 1½" × 6½"

6 strips, 2½" × 42"; crosscut into 140 rectangles, 1½" × 2½"

1 strip, 10½" × 42"; crosscut into 26 sashing rectangles, 1½" × 10½"

17 strips, 1½" × 42"; crosscut 1 of the strips into 2 sashing rectangles, 1½" × 10½"

From each of the 17 assorted red, green, and black print fat quarters, cut:

4 strips, 2½" × 21" (68 total); crosscut each strip into:
    2 rectangles, 2½" × 5" (136 total)
    2 rectangles, 2½" × 3" (136 total)
2 squares, 4½" × 4½" (34 total)

From the red print, cut:

1 square, 4½" × 4½"
4 rectangles, 2½" × 3"
4 rectangles, 2½" × 5"
8 strips, 4½" × 42"
8 binding strips, 2½" × 42"

MAKING THE BLOCKS

After sewing each seam, press the seam allowances in the direction indicated by the arrows.

1. Sew cream 1½" × 4½" rectangles to opposite sides of an assorted print 4½" square; press. Sew cream 1½" × 6½" rectangles to the top and bottom of the square; press.

 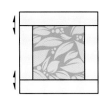

2. Choose four 2½" × 3" rectangles and four 2½" × 5" rectangles from the same print. Sew a cream 1½" × 2½" rectangle between two 2½" × 3" rectangles; press. Make two. Sew these units to the sides of the unit from step 1.

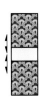 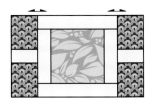

Make 2.

3. Sew a cream 1½" × 2½" rectangle between two 2½" × 5" rectangles; press. Make two. Sew these units to the top and bottom of the unit from step 2.

 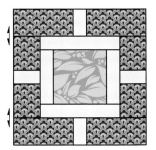

Make 2.

4. Repeat steps 1–3 to make a total of 35 blocks using the remaining fat quarter pieces for 34 blocks and the red-print square and rectangles for one block.

ASSEMBLING THE QUILT TOP

1. Refer to the quilt assembly diagram, opposite, to arrange the blocks in seven horizontal rows of five blocks each, alternating the blocks with the cream 1½" × 10½" sashing rectangles. Sew the blocks and sashing rectangles in each row together. Press the seam allowances open.

2. Cut four cream 1½" × 42" strips in half cross-wise. Sew each half-strip to one end of eight cream 1½" × 42" strips. Trim each of the resulting strips to 54½". Place one of these sashing strips between each of the rows and at the top and bottom of the rows. Sew the block rows and sashing strips together. Press the seam allowances open.

3. Sew two cream 1½" × 42" strips together end to end to make one long strip. Make two. Trim each of the resulting strips to 78½". Sew these strips to the sides of the quilt top. Press the seam allowances open.

4. Sew two red-print 4½" × 42" strips together end to end. Make four. From the pieced strips, cut two strips to the length of the quilt top. Sew the strips to the sides of the quilt top. Press the seam allowances toward the border. Trim the remaining two strips to the width of the quilt top. Sew these strips to the top and bottom of the quilt top. Press the seam allowances toward the border.

FINISHING THE QUILT

Layer and baste the top, batting, and backing together. Quilt as desired. Bind the quilt using the red-print 2½"-wide strips.

Quilt assembly

check

Pieced and quilted by Cindy Lammon

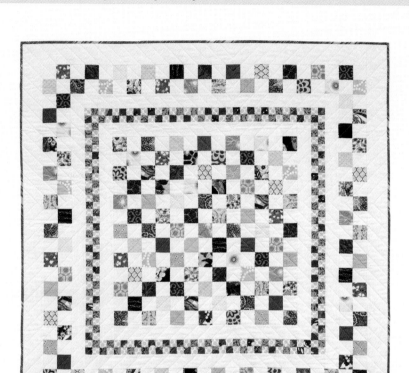

Finished quilt: 52½" x 52½"

This quilt reminds me of a picnic quilt. I grew up in the northeast where winters were long and cold. We sometimes tackled our cabin fever by planning an indoor picnic. Why not throw a quilt on the floor and have a holiday picnic of cookies and hot chocolate?

MATERIALS

Yardage is based on 42"-wide fabric. Fat sixteenths measure 4½" x 21".

2⅛ yards of cream solid for pieced center and borders

22 fat sixteenths of assorted red, green, gold, and teal prints for piecing

⅓ yard of green print for pieced second border

⅓ yard of red print #1 for pieced second border

½ yard of red print #2 for binding

3⅔ yards of fabric for backing

59" x 59" piece of batting

CUTTING

From *each* of the 22 assorted red, green, gold, and teal print fat sixteenths, cut:
1 strip, 2½" x 21" (22 total)

From the cream solid, cut:
11 strips, 2½" x 42"; crosscut in half to make 22 strips, 2½" x 21"
8 strips, 2½" x 42"; crosscut into:
    2 strips, 2½" x 26½"
    2 strips, 2½" x 30½"
    2 strips, 2½" x 34½"
    2 strips, 2½" x 38½"
6 strips, 3½" x 42"

Continued on page 48.

From the green print, cut:
5 strips, 1½" × 42"

From red print #1, cut:
5 strips, 1½" × 42"

From red print #2, cut:
6 binding strips, 2½" × 42"

ASSEMBLING THE QUILT CENTER

After sewing each seam, press the seam allowances in the direction indicated by the arrows.

1. Choose one assorted-print 2½" × 21" strip and crosscut one 2½" square from it. Set the square aside.

2. Sew each assorted-print 2½" × 21" strip, including the leftover strip from step 1, to a cream 2½" × 21" strip along the long edges; press. Make 22 strip sets. Square up the short end of each strip set. Crosscut the strips sets into 168 segments, 2½" wide.

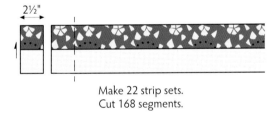

Make 22 strip sets.
Cut 168 segments.

3. Sew 13 segments from step 2 together as shown. Repeat to make a total of six rows. Press the seam allowances toward the right on three of the rows and toward the left on the remaining three rows.

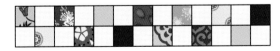

Make 6 rows.

4. Sew six segments from step 2 together end to end, alternating print and cream squares. Add the 2½" square from step 1 to the end of the row. Press the seam allowances toward

the left. Set the remaining segments from step 1 aside for the pieced fourth border.

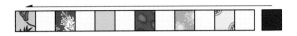

5. Sew the rows from steps 3 and 4 together, alternating rows pressed toward the left and rows pressed toward the right.

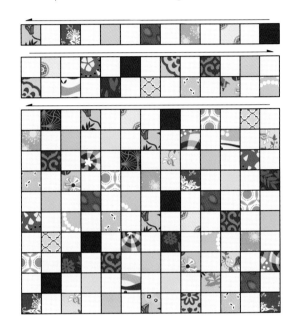

MAKING THE PIECED SECOND-BORDER STRIPS

1. Sew a 1½" × 42" green-print strip to a 1½" × 42" red-print #1 strip along the long edges; press. Repeat to make a total of five strip sets. Square up one end of each strip set. Crosscut the strip sets into 128 segments, 1½" wide.

Make 5 strip sets.
Cut 128 segments.

2. Sew 30 segments together as shown to make a side border strip. Make two. Sew 34 segments together as shown to make a top

Check

border. Repeat for the bottom border. Press the seam allowances open.

Side border.
Make 2.

Top/bottom border.
Make 2.

MAKING THE PIECED FOURTH BORDER STRIPS

Use the segments remaining from the quilt center to make the pieced fourth border strips. Make two side borders using 19 segments each and two borders for the top and bottom using 23 segments each. Press the seam allowances open.

Side border.
Make 2.

Top/bottom border.
Make 2.

ASSEMBLING THE QUILT TOP

1. Refer to the quilt assembly diagram at right to sew the cream 2½" × 26½" strips to the sides of the quilt center. Press the seam allowances toward the strips. Sew the cream 2½" × 30½" strips to the top and bottom of the quilt center. Press the seam allowances toward the strips.

2. Sew the pieced second-border side strips to the sides of the quilt top. Press the seam allowances toward the first border. Sew the pieced second-border top and bottom strips to the top and bottom of the quilt top. Press the seam allowances toward the first border.

3. Sew the cream 2½" × 34½" strips to the sides of the quilt top. Press the seam

allowances toward the newly added strips. Sew the cream 2½" × 38½" strips to the top and bottom of the quilt top. Press the seam allowances toward the newly added strips.

4. Sew the pieced fourth-border side strips to the sides of the quilt top. Press the seam allowances toward the third border. Sew the pieced fourth-border top and bottom strips to the top and bottom of the quilt top. Press the seam allowances toward the third border.

5. Sew three cream 3½" × 42" strips together end to end to make one long strip. Make two. From one of the pieced strips, cut two strips, 3½" × 46½". Sew the strips to the sides of the quilt top. Press the seam allowances toward the newly added strips. From the remaining pieced strip, cut two strips, 3½" × 52½". Sew these strips to the top and bottom of the quilt top. Press the seam allowances toward the newly added strips.

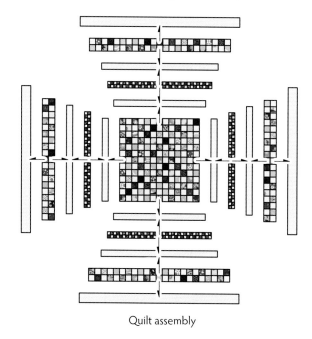

Quilt assembly

FINISHING THE QUILT

Layer and baste the top, batting, and backing together. Quilt as desired. Bind the quilt using the 2½"-wide red-print #2 strips.

stockings

Made by Cindy Lammon

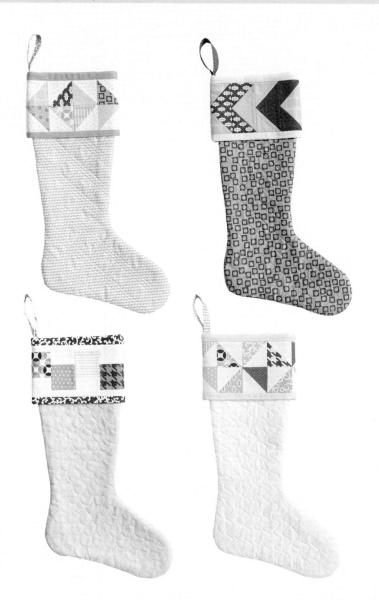

MATERIALS

Yardage is based on 42"-wide fabric and is sufficient for one stocking.

½ yard of print or solid fabric for outer stocking

½ yard of print or solid fabric for stocking lining

¼ yard of print or solid fabric for cuff lining and bands

¼ yard *total* of assorted print and solid scraps, including reds, white, and greens, for pieced cuff

⅝ yard of fusible fleece

Pattern tracing material

Finished stocking: 11" x 20" (across widest and longest points)

In our family, everyone looks forward to peeking inside their stocking for some little goodies. We try to keep the stocking stuffers very personal—a favorite candy, a special writing instrument, or some little gadget. I continue to use my mom's technique of filling up the stocking toe—everyone gets an orange!

CUTTING

For each stocking

From the fusible fleece, cut:
1 rectangle, 5¼" × 16¼"

From the stocking lining fabric, cut:
1 strip, 2" × 8"

From the cuff lining fabric, cut:
1 strip, 6¼" × 16½"
1 strip, 1¼" × 16½"

For the Shifting Squares Cuff

From the assorted print and solid scraps, cut a *total* of:
8 squares, 2½" × 2½"

From the white solid, cut:
8 rectangles, 2" × 2½"
8 rectangles, 1" × 2½"

For the Pinwheels Cuff

From the assorted prints and solid scraps, cut a *total* of:
8 squares, 3" × 3"; cut in half diagonally to yield 16 triangles

From the white solid, cut:
8 squares, 3" × 3"; cut in half diagonally to yield 16 triangles

For the Chevron Cuff

From *each* of 2 red prints and 2 green prints, cut:
2 rectangles, 2½" × 4½" (4 red and 4 green total)
4 squares, 2½" × 2½" (8 red and 8 green total)

For the Triangles and Squares Cuff

From the assorted prints, cut a *total* of:
8 squares, 3" × 3"; cut in half diagonally to yield 16 triangles

From the white solid, cut:
8 squares, 3" × 3"; cut in half diagonally to yield 16 triangles

QUILTING THE OUTER STOCKING

1. Follow the manufacturer's instructions to fuse the *remainder* of the fleece to the wrong side of the outer stocking fabric.

2. Trace the stocking pattern on pages 56–58 onto the pattern tracing material, connecting them to make a complete pattern. Use the pattern to roughly trace one stocking shape and one reverse shape onto the right side of the outer stocking fabric. This will give you a rough quilting area, so that you're not quilting more than needed.

3. Machine quilt the outer stocking fabric. You'll be quilting through the outer fabric and fleece only. Use any quilting design you'd like, or follow one of my designs below.

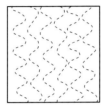 

 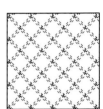

4. Place the stocking pattern back over the quilted fabric and trace one stocking pattern shape and one reverse stocking shape. Cut out the shapes on the drawn lines.

MAKING THE PIECED CUFF

After sewing each seam, press the seam allowances in the direction indicated by the arrows.

Shifting Squares Cuff

1. Sew a white 2" × 2½" rectangle and a white 1" × 2½" rectangle to opposite sides of a print or solid 2½" square; press. Repeat to make a total of eight units.

Make 8.

2. Sew the units from step 1 together in a row, alternating the smaller and larger white rectangles along the top of the strip as shown; press.

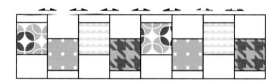

Pinwheels Cuff

1. Sew each white triangle to a print or solid triangle along the long edges to make 16 half-square-triangle units; press. Refer to "Trimming Half-Square-Triangle Units" on page 10 to trim each unit to 2½" × 2½".

Make 16.

2. Sew two units from step 1 together as shown; press. Repeat to make a total of eight pairs.

Make 8.

3. Sew the pairs of half-square-triangle units from step 2 together as shown; press.

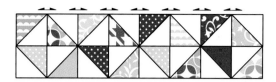

Chevron Cuff

1. Alternately arrange the four red and four green rectangles side by side in a pleasing order. Pair up each rectangle with two squares that match the rectangle fabric to the left. For the rectangle on the far left, match the squares with the rectangle on the far right.

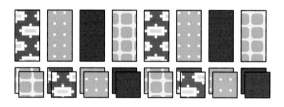

2. Refer to "Flying Geese" on page 9 to make eight flying-geese units using the rectangle and square combinations determined in step 1.

3. Arrange the flying-geese units in the order determined in step 1. Sew the units together along the long edges; press.

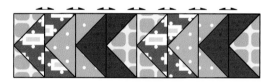

Triangles and Squares Cuff

1. Sew each white triangle to a print triangle along the long edges to make 16 half-square-triangle units; press. Refer to "Trimming Half-Square-Triangle Units" on page 10 to trim each unit to 2½" × 2½".

Make 16.

2. Sew two half-square-triangle units from step 1 together as shown. Repeat to make a total of eight pairs. Press the seam allowances in one direction on four pairs and in the opposite direction on the remaining four pairs.

Make 8.

3. Sew the units from step 2 together as shown, alternating the direction of the seam allowances of each unit so they nest together when sewn; press.

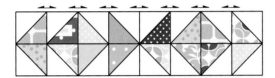

FINISHING THE STOCKING

Use ¼"-wide seam allowances throughout.

1. Sew a cuff-lining 1¼" × 16½" strip to the top of the pieced cuff section and a cuff-lining 6¼" × 16¼" strip to the bottom. Press the seam allowances toward the lining.

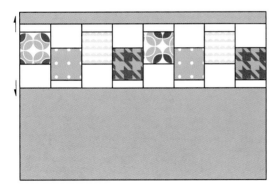

2. Press the cuff in half lengthwise, wrong sides together. Open it back up and fuse the fleece 5¼" × 16¼" rectangle to the wrong side of the pieced half, positioning the rectangle ⅛" from the upper raw edge.

3. Stitch in the ditch along the seam between the pieced section and the lining strips, stitching through the pieced cuff and fleece layers only.

4. With right sides together, sew the short ends of the cuff together. Press the seam allowances open. Fold the lining up along the previously pressed crease, matching the raw edges. Stitch ⅛" from the raw edge.

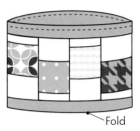

Fold

5. With right sides together, sew the outer stocking pieces together, leaving the top open. Clip the curves and turn the stocking right side out; press flat.

6. Use the stocking pattern to cut one stocking shape and one reverse stocking shape from the lining fabric. With right sides together, sew the lining pieces together, leaving the top open. Do not turn it right side out.

7. Slip the lining into the outer stocking, wrong sides together. Stitch the pieces together ⅛" from the top raw edge.

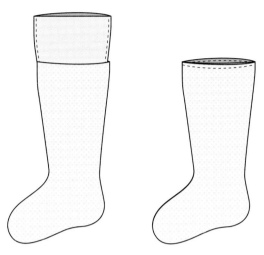

8. To make a hanging loop, press the stocking-lining 2" × 8" strip in half lengthwise, wrong sides together. Open up the strip and fold the long edges in toward the center crease. Refold along the center crease and press. Stitch ⅛" from the folded edges. Fold the strip in half crosswise, with the raw edges on the inside, to make a loop. Place the loop on the lining side of the stocking, matching the raw edges with the heel-side seam; stitch in place.

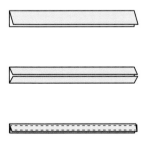

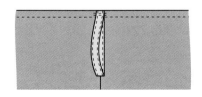

9. Place the cuff inside the stocking with the pieced side toward the lining and the raw edges aligned. Match the cuff seam to the heel-side seam. Stitch around the top of the stocking. To finish the seam allowances, stitch again using a wide zigzag stitch. Turn the cuff to the outside.

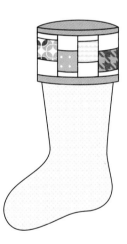

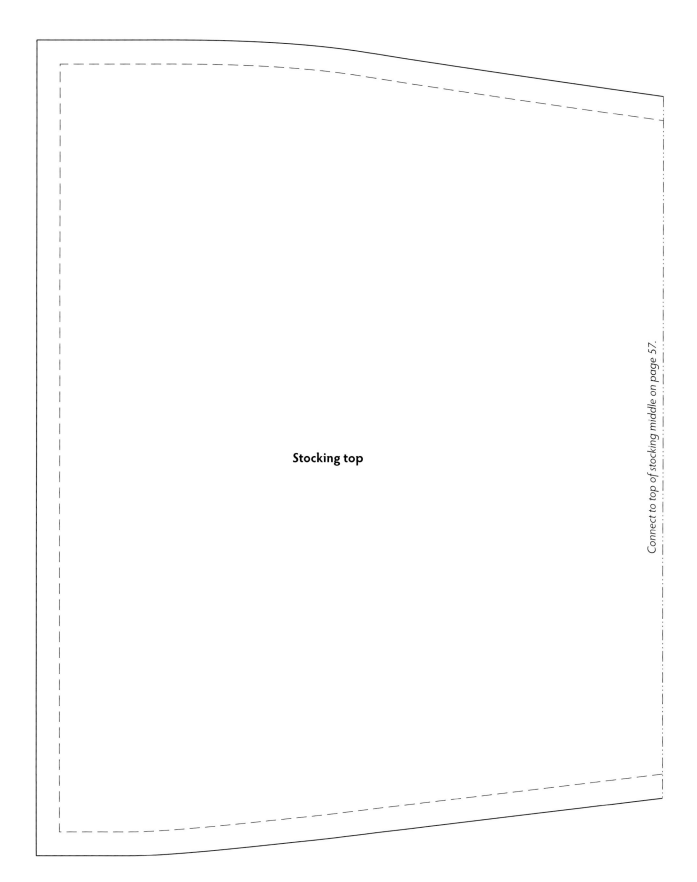

Stocking top

Connect to top of stocking middle on page 57.

Connect to bottom of stocking top on page 56.

Connect to top of stocking heel on page 58.

Stocking middle

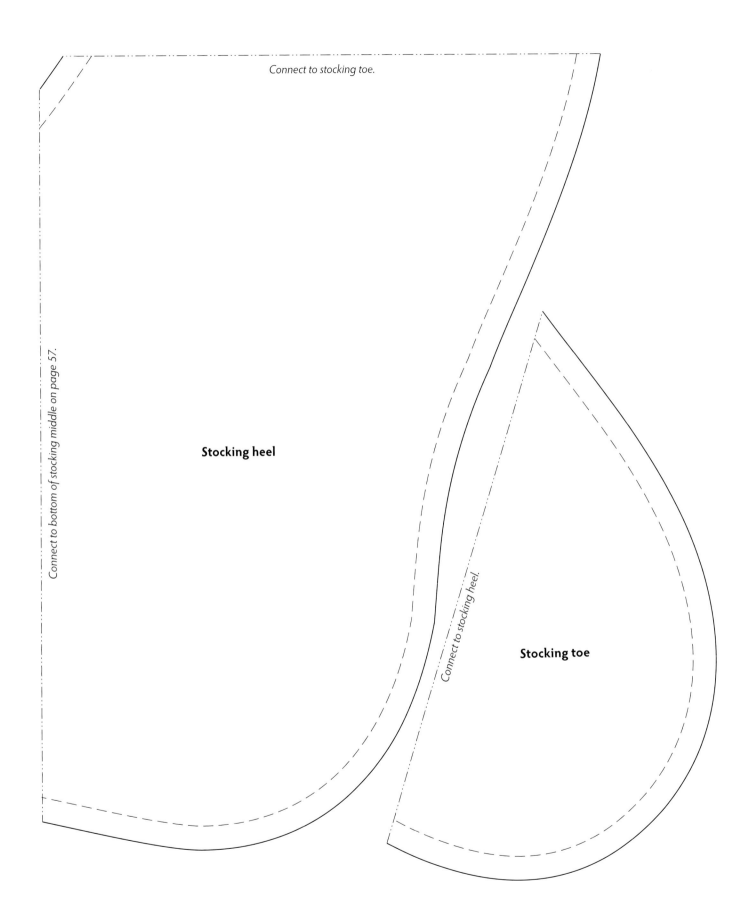

Connect to stocking toe.

Connect to bottom of stocking middle on page 57.

Stocking heel

Connect to stocking heel.

Stocking toe

Stockings

skirted

Pieced and quilted by Cindy Lammon

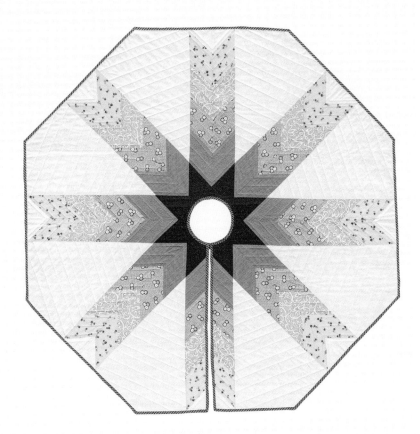

Finished tree skirt: 51" x 51" (across widest and longest points)

Don't let the diamonds in this tree skirt trick you into thinking it's difficult to piece. There are no set-in pieces, making this a quick and easy project. Make one for yourself and maybe one for a lucky recipient on your Christmas list!

MATERIALS

Yardage is based on 42"-wide fabric.

1⅓ yards of white solid for background

⅜ yard *each* of light-red, gray, green, and aqua prints for diamond strips

¼ yard of dark-red print for diamond strips

¾ yard of red print for bias binding

3½ yards of fabric for backing

57" × 57" piece of batting

CUTTING

From the dark-red print, cut:

2 strips, 3½" × 42"; crosscut *1 of the strips* into 1 rectangle, 3½" × 10"

From *each* of the light-red, gray, green, and aqua prints, cut:

3 strips, 3½" × 42"; crosscut *1 strip of each color* into 2 rectangles, 3½" × 10"

From the white solid, cut:

1 strip, 3⅞" × 42"; crosscut into 8 squares, 3⅞" × 3⅞". Cut each square in half diagonally to yield 16 triangles.

4 squares, 18" × 18"; cut in half diagonally to yield 8 triangles

From the *bias* of the red print, cut:

Enough 2½"-wide strips to equal 250" when sewn together end to end

MAKING THE TREE SKIRT

1. Sew a dark-red 3½" × 42" strip to a light-red 3½" × 42" strip as shown, offsetting the strip by approximately 3". Add the gray, green, and aqua strips in the same manner, offsetting each one by 3". Press the seam allowances toward the dark-red strip.

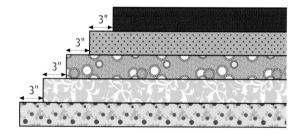

2. Repeat step 1 using the 3½" × 10" rectangles.

3. Sew a light-red 3½" × 42" strip to a gray 3½" × 42" strip, offsetting the strips by approximately 3". Add the green and aqua strips in the same manner. Notice that these strips are staggered in the opposite direction

from the strip sets in steps 1 and 2. Press the seam allowances toward the aqua strip.

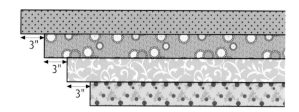

4. Repeat step 3 using the 3½" × 10" strips.

5. Align the 45° angle line of a ruler on a seam line of the strip set from step 1, following the direction of the stacking. Trim and discard the end. Align the 3½" line of the ruler on the newly trimmed edge and cut a segment 3½" wide. Continue cutting across the strip to cut as many 3½"-wide segments as possible. Repeat with the strip set from step 2, cutting a total of eight segments from the two strip sets.

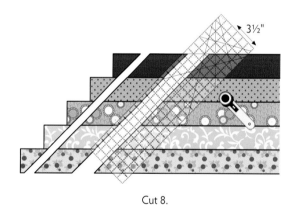

Cut 8.

6. Repeat step 5 using the strip sets from steps 3 and 4, angling the ruler in the opposite direction.

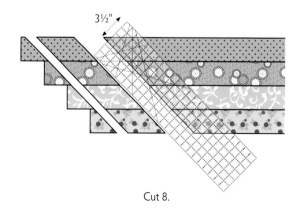

Cut 8.

7. Sew the long edge of a small white half-square triangle to the aqua diamond on the end of each segment from steps 5 and 6. Press the seam allowances in the same direction as the diamonds on each segment.

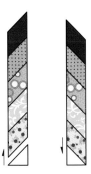

8. Align the long edge of a large white half-square triangle with the long edge of a four-diamond segment, positioning the segments so that a small tip of the large white triangle is exposed. The point of the V formed should be ¼" from the edge. The white triangle is oversized, so it will be longer than the diamond strip. Pin and then sew the strip to the triangle. Press the seam allowances open. Repeat to make a total of eight units.

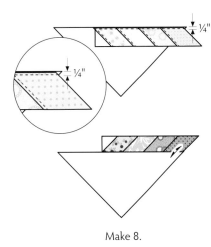

Make 8.

9. Align a five-diamond segment along the side adjacent to the four-diamond segment of a unit from step 8, positioning it so that a small tip of the light-red diamond hangs over the end. The point of the V formed should be ¼" from the edge. Pin and then sew the strip

in place. Press the seam allowances open. Repeat to make a total of eight units.

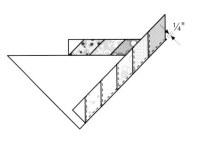

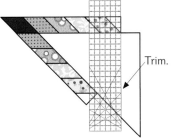

Make 8.

10. Use your ruler and a rotary cutter to trim off the excess of the large white triangle from each unit from step 9, trimming it even with the small white triangles.

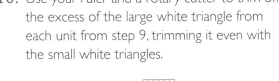

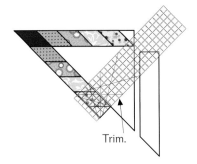

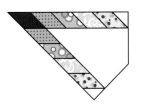

11. Sew the units from step 10 together in pairs, and then sew the pairs into halves. Press the seam allowances open.

12. Sew the halves together, using a basting stitch from the center to one edge for one seam. Mark the basted seam with a small piece of masking tape placed along the edge—you'll remove the basting stitches after quilting to open up the tree skirt.

Masking tape

Tree-skirt assembly

FINISHING THE TREE SKIRT

1. Draw a 6"-diameter circle in the center of the tree skirt. Piece the backing. Layer and baste the top, batting, and backing together. Quilt as desired, avoiding the center circle and the basted seam.

2. Trim the edges of the backing even with the tree skirt. Remove the stitches of the basted seam and trim off the ¼" seam allowances.

Open basted seam
and trim seam allowances.

3. Make an opening for the tree skirt by cutting the batting and the backing at the open seam and cutting out the marked circle.

4. Bind the tree skirt using the red-print 2½"-wide bias binding.

snowball games

Pieced and quilted by Cindy Lammon

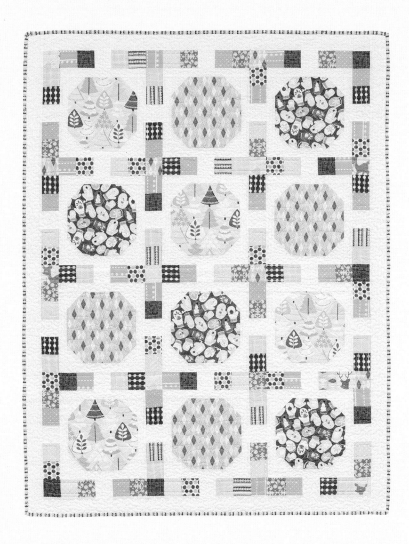

Finished quilt: 42½" x 54½" * Finished block: 10" x 10"

How about a Christmas quilt for a little one in your life? The Snowball blocks in this project offer a great opportunity to showcase a wonderful novelty print. Of course, this would be a quick and easy kid's quilt for any time of the year!

MATERIALS

Yardage is based on 42"-wide fabric. Fat eighths measure 9" x 21".

1⅓ yards of white solid for background

⅓ yard *each* of 3 assorted novelty prints for Snowball blocks

9 fat eighths of assorted red, green, and aqua prints for sashing

½ yard of multicolor-striped fabric for sashing and binding

3 yards of fabric for backing

49" x 61" piece of batting

CUTTING

From *each* of the 3 assorted novelty prints, cut:
4 squares, 8½" × 8½" (12 total)

From the white solid, cut:
12 strips, 1½" × 42"; crosscut *each* strip into:
    2 rectangles, 1½" × 10½" (24 total)
    2 rectangles, 1½" × 8½" (24 total)
10 strips, 2½" × 42"; crosscut *5 of the strips* into
    79 squares, 2½" × 2½"

From *each* of the 9 assorted red-, green-, and aqua-print fat eighths, cut:
2 strips, 2½" × 21" (18 total); crosscut *3 of the strips* into 20 squares 2½" × 2½"

From the multicolor-striped fabric, cut:
1 strip, 2½" × 21"
5 binding strips, 2½" × 42"

MAKING THE BLOCKS

After sewing each seam, press the seam allowances in the direction indicated by the arrows.

1. Use your preferred marker to draw a diagonal line from corner to corner on the wrong side of four white 2½" squares. Place a marked square on each corner of a novelty print 8½" square, noting the direction of the marked line. Sew on the marked line. Trim ¼" from the stitching line; press. Repeat to make a total of 12 units.

Make 12.

2. Sew white 1½" × 8½" rectangles to opposite sides of each unit from step 1; press. Sew white 1½" × 10½" rectangles to the top and bottom of each unit; press.

Make 12.

MAKING THE SASHING UNITS

1. Using the assorted red-, green-, or aqua-print and multicolor-striped 2½" × 21" strips, sew two different strips together along the long edges to make a strip set; press. Repeat to make a total of eight strip sets. Crosscut the strip sets into 62 segments, 2½" wide.

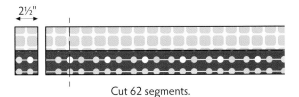

Cut 62 segments.

2. Sew a white 2½" square between two of the segments from step 1; press. Repeat to make a total of 31 sashing units.

Make 31.

ASSEMBLING THE QUILT TOP

1. Refer to the quilt assembly diagram below to arrange the blocks, sashing units, and remaining 20 red-, green-, or aqua-print 2½" squares as shown. Sew the sashing units and squares in each sashing row together. Press the seam allowances toward the squares. Sew the blocks and sashing units in each block row together. Press the seam allowances toward the blocks. Sew the block and sashing rows together. Press the seam allowances open.

2. Trim two white 2½" × 42" strips to the width of the quilt top. Sew the strips to the top and bottom of the quilt top. Press the seam allowances toward the border. Sew the remaining three white 2½" × 42" strips together end to end to make one long strip. From the pieced strip, cut two strips to the length of the quilt top. Sew these strips to the sides of the quilt top. Press the seam allowances toward the border.

FINISHING THE QUILT

Layer and baste the top, batting, and backing together. Quilt as desired. Bind the quilt using the multicolor-striped 2½"-wide strips.

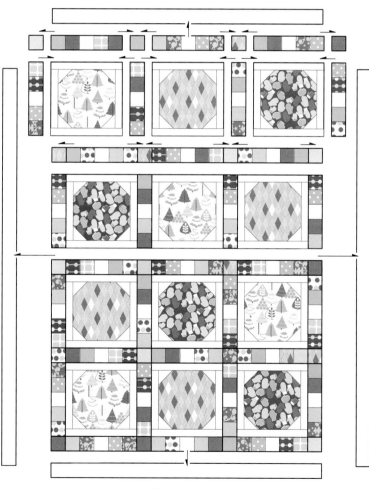

Quilt assembly

hanging around

Pieced and machine quilted by Cindy Lammon

Finished table topper: 28½" x 28½"

Wreaths are such a traditional holiday decoration. I love the idea of a simple, modern wreath ready to grace the table. The center is left plain so you can add a beautiful holiday centerpiece!

MATERIALS

Yardage is based on 42"-wide fabric.

1⅛ yards of white solid for background

½ yard *total* of assorted green prints for piecing

⅓ yard of red-and-white striped fabric for binding

1⅛ yards of fabric for backing

34" x 34" piece of batting

CUTTING

From the white solid, cut:

1 strip, 12½" × 42"; crosscut into 1 square, 12½" × 12½". Trim the remainder of the strip to 4½" wide; crosscut into 4 rectangles, 4½" × 6½".

3 strips, 3" × 42"; crosscut into 30 squares, 3" × 3". Cut each square in half diagonally to yield 60 triangles.

1 strip, 4½" × 42"; crosscut into 12 rectangles, 2½" × 4½"

2 strips, 2½" × 24½"

2 strips, 2½" × 28½"

From the assorted green prints, cut a *total* of:

4 squares, 4½" × 4½"

30 squares, 3" × 3"; cut in half diagonally to yield 60 triangles

From the red-and-white striped fabric, cut:

3 binding strips, 2½" × 42"

MAKING THE BLOCKS

After sewing each seam, press the seam allowances in the direction indicated by the arrows.

1. Use your preferred marker to draw a diagonal line from corner to corner on the wrong side of four green 4½" squares. Place a marked square on each corner of the white 12½" square, noting the direction of the marked lines. Sew on the marked line. Trim ¼" from the stitching line; press.

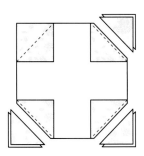 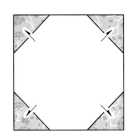

2. Sew a green triangle to a white triangle along the long edges; press. Repeat to make a total of 60 half-square-triangle units. Refer to "Trimming Half-Square-Triangle Units" on page 10 to trim the units to 2½" × 2½".

Make 60.

3. Sew six half-square-triangle units together as shown to make row A; press. Repeat to make a total of eight rows.

Row A.
Make 8.

4. Sew two half-square triangle units together as shown. Sew a white 2½" × 4½" rectangle to each end to make row B; press. Repeat to make a total of four rows.

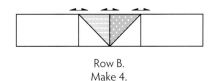

Row B.
Make 4.

5. Sew two A rows and one B row together as shown; press. Repeat to make a total of four side units.

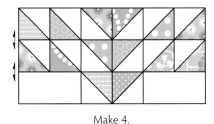

Make 4.

6. Sew one of the remaining half-square-triangle units to a white 2½" × 4½" rectangle; press. Sew a white 4½" × 6½" rectangle to the bottom of this unit; press. Repeat to make a total of four corner units.

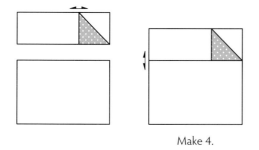

Make 4.

ASSEMBLING THE TABLE TOPPER TOP

1. Refer to the table-topper assembly diagram below to arrange the side units and corner units into three horizontal rows as shown. Sew the units in each row together; press. Join the rows; press.

2. Sew the white 2½" × 24½" strips to the sides of the table-topper top; press. Sew the white 2½" × 28½" strips to the top and bottom of the table-topper top; press.

FINISHING THE TABLE TOPPER

Layer and baste the top, batting, and backing together. Quilt as desired. Bind the table topper using the red-and-white striped 2½"-wide strips.

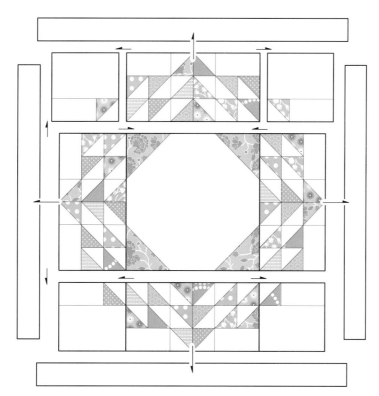

Table-topper assembly

simply simple

Pieced and machine quilted by Cindy Lammon

Finished table runner: 15½" x 38½"

Several years ago I designed a table runner for one of our local quilt shops and called it "Simply Simple." It was such a popular pattern because it was, well, simple. I've actually simplified it even more and left the ends without a border treatment so that you can easily change the length. I guarantee you'll make this one over and over again. Couldn't be simpler!

MATERIALS

Yardage is based on 42"-wide fabric.

⅓ yard of large-scale print for center

¼ yard of white solid for inner and outer borders

⅛ yard of red solid for pieced middle border

4" x 12" rectangle *each* of 5 green and gray prints *total* for pieced middle border

⅓ yard of green print for binding

⅔ yard of fabric for backing*

20" x 42" piece of batting

*If the backing fabric doesn't measure 42" wide after it's been washed, you'll need 1⅓ yards.

CUTTING

From the red solid, cut:

2 strips, 1" × 42"; crosscut into 5 rectangles, 1" × 9"

From *each of 3* of the green and/or gray prints, cut:

1 rectangle, 3½" × 9" (3 total)

From *each of the remaining 2* green and/or gray prints, cut:

1 rectangle, 3½" × 9" (2 total)
1 rectangle, 2" × 3½" (2 total)

From the white solid, cut:

4 strips, 1½" × 38½"

From the large-scale print, cut:

1 strip, 8½" × 38½"

From the green print, cut:

3 binding strips, 2½" × 42"

MAKING THE TABLE RUNNER

After sewing each seam, press the seam allowances in the direction indicated by the arrows.

1. Sew a red rectangle to each of the five green and/or gray print 3½" × 9" rectangles along the long edges to make a strip set; press. Square up the short end of each strip set and crosscut each one into four segments, 2" wide (20 total).

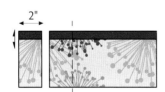

Make 5 strip sets.
Cut 4 segments from each (20 total).

2. Randomly sew 10 segments together along the short edges as shown, making sure the green and gray rectangles alternate with the red rectangles. Sew one of the remaining gray or green 2" × 3½" rectangles to the red rectangle at the end of the strip; press. Repeat to make a total of two strips.

Make 2.

3. Sew a white strip to each side of the pieced rows; press the seam allowances open.

4. Sew the borders from step 3 to the long edges of the large-scale print strip.

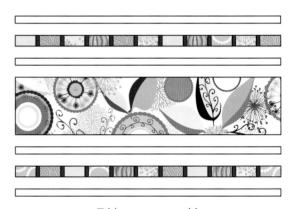

Table-runner assembly

FINISHING THE TABLE RUNNER

Layer and baste the top, batting, and backing together. Quilt as desired. Bind the table runner using the green 2½"-wide strips.

Quilt It Simply!

I quilted my table runner with straight-line rows of stitching about ½" apart. This may look like a lot of work, but it actually goes very quickly. Use the edge of your walking foot as a guide for spacing. The effect is really nice and it's super simple.

coming together

Pieced and machine quilted by Cindy Lammon

Finished quilt: 60½" x 60½"

No one will argue that the best part of the season is when families and friends come together to worship, celebrate, and enjoy each others' company. This quilt is pretty simple, made primarily of flying-geese units. I like to think they're all flying home.

MATERIALS

Yardage is based on 42"-wide fabric. Fat eighths measure 9" x 21".

2⅛ yards of white solid for background

1⅛ yards of multicolored print for large squares

¾ yard of medium-green print for quarter-square-triangle units and outer border

⅓ yard of white polka-dot print for medium squares

¼ yard of light-green print for quarter-square-triangle units

11 fat eighths of assorted red prints for flying-geese units

10 fat eighths of assorted green prints for flying-geese units

⅝ yard of red polka-dot print for binding

4⅛ yards of fabric for backing

66" x 66" piece of batting

CUTTING

From *each* of the 10 green-print fat eighths, cut:
1 strip, 4½" × 21"; crosscut into 8 rectangles,
    2½" × 4½" (80 total)

From *each* of the 11 red-print fat eighths, cut:
1 strip, 4½" × 21"; crosscut into 8 rectangles,
    2½" × 4½" (88 total)

From the remainder of 1 red-print fat eighth, cut:
4 squares, 2½" × 2½"

From the white solid, cut:
27 strips, 2½" × 42"; crosscut *12 of the strips* into:
    336 squares, 2½" × 2½"
    4 rectangles, 2½" × 20½"
    8 rectangles, 2½" × 12½"

From the medium-green print, cut:
1 strip, 5¼" × 42"; crosscut into 7 squares,
    5¼" × 5¼". Cut each square into quarters
    diagonally to yield 28 triangles (you'll have
    2 left over).
7 strips, 2½" × 42"

From the light-green print, cut:
1 strip, 5¼" × 42"; crosscut into 7 squares,
    5¼" × 5¼". Cut each square into quarters
    diagonally to yield 28 triangles (you'll have
    2 left over).

From the multicolored print, cut:
4 strips, 8½" × 42"; crosscut into 16 squares,
    8½" × 8½"

From the white polka-dot print, cut:
2 strips, 4½" × 42"; crosscut into 12 squares,
    4½" × 4½"

From the red polka-dot print, cut:
7 binding strips, 2½" × 42"

MAKE THE FLYING-GEESE UNITS

After sewing each seam, press the seam allowances
in the direction indicated by the arrows.

1. Refer to "Flying Geese" on page 9 to make 80
    flying-geese units using the green 2½" × 4½"
    rectangles and the white 2½" squares. Make
    88 flying-geese units using the red 2½" × 4½"
    rectangles and the remaining white 2½" squares.

Make 80.   Make 88.

2. Sew two red and two green flying-geese units
    together along the long edges, alternating
    the colors as shown; press. Repeat to make
    a total of 40 units. You'll have eight red flying-
    geese units left over.

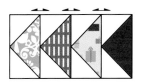

Make 40.

MAKING THE QUARTER-SQUARE-TRIANGLE UNITS

Sew a light-green triangle to a medium-green triangle along the short sides; press. Repeat to make
a total of 26 pairs. Sew two units together along
the long edges as shown; press.

Make 13.

ASSEMBLING THE QUILT

1. Refer to the quilt assembly diagram below to arrange the flying-geese units, quarter-square-triangle units, white polka-dot 4½" squares, and multicolored 8½" squares into rows. Sew the pieces in each row together. Press the seam allowances away from the flying-geese units. Join the rows; press the seam allowances toward the multicolored-square rows.

2. Join two white 2½" x 12½" rectangles, one white 2½" x 20½" rectangle, and two red flying-geese units as shown. Repeat to make a total of four strips. Press the seam allowances of two strips toward the rectangles and those of the remaining two strips toward the flying-geese units.

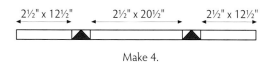

Make 4.

3. Sew two strips from step 2 with the seam allowances pressed toward the flying-geese units to the sides of the quilt top; press. Sew a red 2½" square to the ends of the remaining two strips from step 2. Sew these strips to the top and bottom of the quilt top; press.

4. Sew three medium-green 2½" x 42" strips together end to end to make one long strip. From the pieced strip, cut two strips the length of the quilt top. Sew the strips to the sides of the quilt top; press. Sew two medium-green 2½" x 42" strips together end to end. Repeat to make a total of two pieced strips. Trim each pieced strip to the width of the quilt top. Sew these strips to the top and bottom of the quilt top; press.

FINISHING THE QUILT

Layer and baste the top, batting, and backing together. Quilt as desired. Bind the quilt using the red polka-dot 2½"-wide strips.

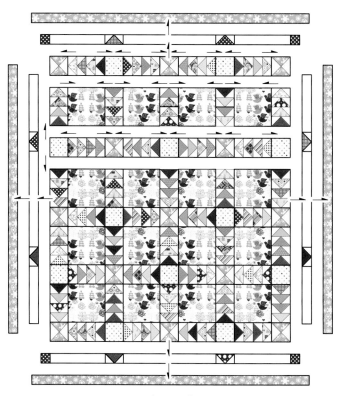

Quilt assembly

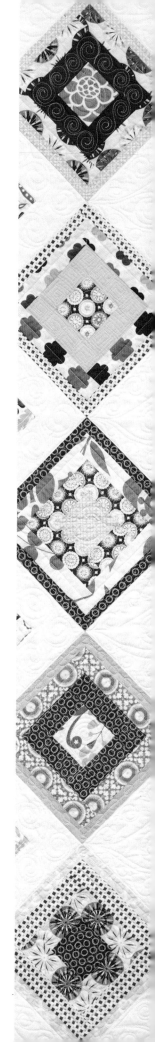

acknowledgments

Thank you to some wonderful friends and sewists who helped with several quilts: Wynema Bean, Jean Maiuro, Rene Shoults, and Bonnie Forsee.

Special thanks to my husband, Mike, for doing all the things required of a quilter's husband and always doing them with a smile.

about the author

Cindy Lammon began sewing at her mother's and grandmother's side as a small child. She took a beginner quilting class in 1981 and started what would become a life-long passion for fabric, quilting, crafting, and handwork. She began teaching and designing quilts while working at a local quilt shop. This is her fourth book with Martingale.

In addition to quilting, Cindy loves gardening, decorating, and reading. And she's recently taken on the challenge of creative photography. For Cindy, the next step is to carry on the sewing tradition with her own granddaughters!